C000020051

A SPILLAGE OF MERCURY

A SPILLAGE OF MERCURY

Neil Rollinson

CAPE POETRY

First published 1996

1 3 5 7 9 10 8 6 4 2

© Neil Rollinson 1996

Neil Rollinson has asserted his right
under the Copyright, Designs and Patents Act, 1988
to be identified as the author of this work

First published in the United Kingdom in 1996 by
Jonathan Cape
Random House, 20 Vauxhall Bridge Road, London SW1V 2SA

Random House Australia (Pty) Limited
20 Alfred Street, Milsons Point, Sydney,
New South Wales 2061, Australia

Random House New Zealand Limited
18 Poland Road, Glenfield,
Auckland 10, New Zealand

Random House South Africa (Pty) Limited
PO Box 337, Bergvlei, South Africa

Random House UK Limited Reg. No. 954009

A CIP catalogue record for this book
is available from the British Library
ISBN 0–224–04008–1

Phototypeset by Intype London Ltd
Printed and bound in Great Britain by
Mackays of Chatham PLC

For Louise
and for
Matthew

CONTENTS

ACKNOWLEDGEMENTS

Acknowledgements are due to the following: *London Magazine*, *The New Yorker*, *The North*, *Observer*, *Poetry London Newsletter*, *London Review of Books*, *Resurgence*, *The Rialto*, *Smiths Knoll*, *Stand*.

'The Rains that Never Fell' won third prize in the South West Poetry Competition, 1993, and 'The Blowing of Birds' Eggs' won second prize in the same competition in 1994. 'The Garden' won third prize in the Keithley Poetry Competition in 1995. 'The Way it Happens' won a prize in the *Observer* Arvon International Poetry Competition of 1995.

Thanks go to the following for their help and encouragement: Matthew Sweeney, Robin Robertson, John Moat, John Fairfax, Peter Redgrove, Penny Shuttle, Michael Bayley, Arvon at Totleigh Barton, Sue Stewart, The Poetry Business, Harry Laing, Barry Juniper, Tim Akers, and Louise Clarke. There's a drink at the bar!

LIKE THE BLOWING OF BIRDS' EGGS

I crack the shell
on the bedstead and open it
over your stomach. It runs
to your navel and settles there
like the stone of a sharon fruit.

You ask me to gather it up
and pour it over your breast
without breaking the membrane.

It swims in my palm, drools
from the gaps in my fingers, fragrant,
spotted with blood.

It slips down your chest,
moves on your skin like a woman
hurrying in her yellow dress, the long
transparent train dragging behind.

It slides down your belly and into your
pubic hair where you burst
the yolk with a tap of your finger.

It covers your cunt in a shock
of gold. You tell me to eat,
to feel the sticky glair on my tongue.

I lick the folds of your sex, the coarse
damp hairs, the slopes of your arse
until you're clean, and tense as a clock spring.

I touch your spot and something inside you
explodes like the blowing of birds' eggs.

THE BLUE CANOES

The murmur of stranded drinkers,
roof beams groaning, easing themselves
into the ceiling. A cow goes under
the bridge, its legs stuck up
like the masts of a ship, a car
bubbles on the staith.
The beer's going down fine.

                           The men
in the blue canoes drink casually.
The delivery wagon is stuck
at the top of the road.
We've been here too long,
but what the hell.
The river conducts its cold sleep
through our wellington boots.
We're into that boozy dream
between dozing and sniggering.

                           There goes
the last bottle of beer
with an idle fizz.
The landlord fills his glass,
We're onto the optics now.
I hope this rain stops soon.
The men in the blue canoes
empty their glasses and paddle out.
We watch them as far as Skeldergate Bridge
where the clouds erase them.
Did you see that cow? somebody asks.
Nobody did.

THE RAINS THAT NEVER FELL
FELL IN MY HOUSE

I turn on the tap, the drain belches.
I let it run all night:
a thousand gallons go to the sea.

Soon I'm dissatisfied. I turn on the other tap.
Double sounds twice as good.
I go up the stairs, turn on the bath:
its great cold-water tap gushes wildly, then
the sink's, until the plumbing sings
and the house is a thunder cloud pouring rain.

To think how many could have drunk from this.
How easy to keep death away.

I waste it: as much as I can; king in my own home.
If I had more, I'd squander more, I'd run
the neighbours' taps; the whole street's.
I see a town of sunken cataracts: drains and sewers
glutted with waste water, the suburbs would hiss
beneath the maple trees.
I could say without doubt,
the whole of Africa's rainfall fell in my house tonight.

DESCARTES

Descartes, my latest purchase
from the Pisces Aquarium,
keeps jumping out of his tank
onto the carpet.

Each time, I pick him up
like a spillage of mercury
and drop him back
in his watery world

of bubbles, sunken
bridges and mermaids;
the neons spark like tinder.
But later, he's out again,

a limbless gymnast,
flipping about on the rug.
What does he think,
if he thinks at all, is out here

in this waterless paradise?
He must have some absurd
sense of dissatisfaction, maybe
the living room looks

a more spacious pond,
greener, more full of light,
the armchairs glowing
with subterranean warmth.

What does he hate so much?
Is the world too small for him?

His genes were brewed
in warm South American waters,

I can hardly release him
into the Foss, stickleback
though he resembles, his blood
contains no anti-freeze.

I hold him gently, speak to him,
of common sense, he lies
in my palm like a bit of moonlight,
a dribble of spit. His eyes hold

nothing except the mystery
of carpet pile, bread crumbs,
and the undersides of tables,
his gills opening, closing,

his mouth piping a silent
plea for the Orinoco.
When I leave the room
I can only hope for the best.

Sure enough, when I return
he's laid on the sofa
stiff as a whitebait,
his colour gone, the mucus

dried, his pupils fixed
on the ripples of Artex
coating the ceiling.
It's the toilet for you

my friend, the long journey
to the sea, through cold drainpipes

and sewers, back to the fishy
realms of your cold cousins

nosing the Humber estuary; this
is where curiosity gets you,
the enquiring mind. There is nothing
on the other side of the glass,

except tables and chairs.
I drop him into the toilet bowl,
and somehow, from the depths
of his heart, he summons the will

to swim again, he shivers to life,
but not before the handle
has been engaged. The cistern
erupts and floods from the rim.

He fights the current a moment
then disappears, off where he wants
to be, heading to sea, the smell
of the Orinoco dilating his nostrils.

GIANT PUFFBALLS

Can I make it home, or do I shit
in the woods? I squat above the moss,
breathing its pheromones, my scrotum
shrunk like a walnut in the cold breeze.
I push quietly in case the dogs
on their morning walks come sniffing.
It drops on the leaves
with a muffled thud, and the smell
is like marzipan, not offensive
as it is against the clinical spruce
of the ordinary bathroom. It steams
in the dirt; the undigested sweetcorn
bright as stones in a brooch.
Coconut milk, rice from Shanghai,
spice from Afghanistan,
all remaking itself; feeding the trees.
I clean myself on a sycamore leaf,
smooth as a grocer's handkerchief.
And then I see them: pregnant
as fish bowls, weird as a hedgeful
of skulls. I pull one out of its hole
gentle as a midwife, palping the domed
head in my hands; I carry it home
on the bus; it sits in my lap
like a baby, plump, bald as an arse,
smelling of milk and cinnamon.

THE GARDEN

He's juggling his cutlery over the table
as I bring in the turkey, their flames
twist on the polished top. When he hears me come
he lays the implements in their proper spaces
and carves the breast. He spreads the pieces
on my plate like a cartomancer, carefully,
portentously beside the peas.
I inspect my slices for defects, for signs
of doubt or hesitation, even for errors
of gauge but each carving is clean
as a credit card. After our meal he takes
my arm and leads me through the house
to show me his garden.
                              A summer's day,
a woman raking the lawn, a man
filling his barrow with stones.
What are those birds, I ask, and he stops
for a moment and listens: *a thrush,*
a couple of blackbirds and a robin
up in the alder, he tells me.
We sit on a bench and look at the garden.
See that tree in the middle of the lawn? he asks.
It casts a column of silence across the grass
exactly like a shadow. And he gets up
and strolls by the flowers. I close
my eyes and try to see what he means,
but all I get are the sparks at the backs
of the eyes, and then a woman I know
taking her clothes off. I give up.
Hanging back, I swipe at wasps with his ivory cane;
he wanders on, dead-heading the roses.

SMALL CHANGE

The blind man clocks me with his outstretched
hand. Small change, he says, any small change?
I dig in my trousers, pull out a fist
full of coins, and putting the pounds
back where they came from, pass him the rest.
Fifty-four pence he says, thank you very much.
I circle round and wait for his radar
to pick me up again. Small change, he says
and I fish for the rest of my coins,
this time counting it: thirty-six p.   He grasps
the trouser-warm coins and tests the weight
with a few minute movements – a doctor
checking his patient's testicles.
Thirty-six pence, thanks a lot, and off he goes
like a one-armed dowser sweeping for water.
Someone puts money in his hand, he calculates
the composite weights and announces the sum,
thanks them, and wanders away leaving them
duly suspicious. I stalk him
from Waterloo Bridge to Hungerford Bridge
performing his calculus, a group of tourists
tagging along, cameras snapping.
I solicit a few foreigners to hand over coins
and approach from the side. Small change, he says
when I'm in the cross-hairs. I offer
the shrapnel. Thank you sir, six francs,
four Deutschmarks, two thousand lira, and six
Austrian schillings, very generous, exactly
four pounds and ten pence at the present rate.

FREE FALL

His parachute felt like a satchel
of bricks on his back, he imagined
the canopy furled inside, every crease
and fold in the fabric critical, the rip-cord
beat on his chest like a metronome.
He couldn't get her face out of his mind.
I love you, he thought, I can't let you
watch me rot in a chair.
He was God for a moment, all the fields
and towns laid at his fingertips.
He could hear the plane as it moved away,
then just the rushing of air in his head.
He felt the disease creep through his legs.
As he fell through the sky he could smell
each tree, each of the hundred wild flowers
of Berkshire, the clean, damp scent of salmon
cruising the Thames. He fell through the blue
morning, slicing the endless half distances
he'd read about (a falling ball never reaches
the floor they say: he'd soon find out).
He thought about the bills he'd left,
the Minibels growing sweet in the greenhouse,
his wife's beautiful sad face; he fingered
the rip-cord, thought about pulling, there was
still time, just, but he'd made up his mind.
He remembered Gypsy Lee on their honeymoon
tracing the deep, unbroken life-line
round his thumb: a long and happy life,
she'd said. The world turned green
as he travelled into the lawn of a council
house in Newbury, his mind so fast
he noticed the microscopic details of everything:
the point of a grass blade, the spores

of a mushroom, the head of a garden ant,
he could see his face for a moment in the hundred
facets of its eye as he fell through the roots
of dandelions, buttercups, and the muddy spirals
of worm-holes.

THE LAST BUS TO NOWHERE

As I came round the corner
the bus was just leaving. It was
hot, and I wasn't in a rush,
but something snapped in my head
and I started to run.
As it pulled away and picked up speed
I was full tilt in its slipstream.
White lines flashed below,
sweat bubbled under my hair.
The bus crunched into second gear
as I was moving smoothly
into third, breathing pure diesel,
the trees in the park
flickered by like Super-8 film:
a child hung motionless in a swing.
After fifty metres it was touch and go,
but I'd got to the point of no return,
my legs were sheer motion, I could
see the faces of startled drivers
in the opposite lane.
As the bus lurched into third
I managed to get my hands
on the pole at the back,
but when I jumped, my legs flailed,
I could feel my toe caps
scraping the tarmac.
I clung on tight,
trailing behind
like an earthing-strip,
a diver in mid belly-flop.
The inside of the bus was as calm
as somebody's sitting room, people
were reading the morning papers, listening

to walkmans. I felt weak, the road
rushed under me like rapids,
and with a last almighty effort
I pulled with my arms, got my knees
onto the platform, crawled
on all fours to the first seat in the bus,
and sat there trembling, trying
to sort the change in my pocket.

SUN STROKE

She takes off her clothes and follows the sun
with a slavish obsession
down the back garden with a deckchair,
as if the shadow of the house
might give her a dangerous disease.
When the sun clears the roof she's gone:
sunning herself by the front porch,
the colour of luncheon meat, basting
her melanomas with factor 5. From the cool
of the house, I watch her move
from the rough black shadow of the roof extension,
down to the mown verge of Juniper Close
She spreads herself out between the trees,
squeezing the last dregs
of ultra violet from the bright yellow day.
Mr Barker can't believe his eyes,
he mows his lawn, then mows it again.
When the sun vanishes over the suburbs
there's nowhere else to go,
she gets her dress from the flower-beds,
shakes out the wildlife, and enters the house,
so full of the day's heat
she warms the cool rooms like a human radiator.

CORNUCOPIA

It lies on his thigh, dribbling,
dead to the world. She kisses him,
she's not finished yet; she squeezes
the limp flesh like a pastry cook
between her fingers. He groans.
He's had enough. She takes the slob
of it into her mouth
and tickles the head.
               He grows in spite of himself,
swells in the moist blowhole.
She's good at this, bringing him back again
and again from a premature end.
He'll thank her tomorrow.
She fingers the gonads, they move
and squirm in their sack like a purse
of maggots. She's got him now where she wants him.
It's a two-hand job the third time round,
and when he comes it's barely a spoonful,
froth and bubbles, the mousse
of a good Champagne. She tops
him off with a long sponge of her tongue.
He shrinks again; she kisses the hairs
on his thigh, he thinks that's it.
She rustles about in her bag, pulls out
a rope, a length of silk and a plastic tube
with a pump on the end.

BETWEEN BRADFORD
AND PUDSEY

The long drive home,
the jaundice
of yellow street-lights
gilding the car,
and then
between Bradford
and Pudsey, a frenzy
of white horses
loose from their field,
skating the black road,
drunk as fairground horses,
their eyes wild
in the headlights.
Dad slows to a crawl
at the roundabout,
the horses scatter:
a merry-go-round exploding
in slow motion,
all the horses
off their poles,
an instinct gathers them
and they sprint down
the ring road in a
welter of hoof sparks,
panic driving them
deeper and deeper
into their nightmare:
Thornbury, Laisterdyke,
Dudley Hill.

SWIMMING TO THE WATER TABLE

After hours of silence and the velvet
of peat cloughs, the road
from Manchester cuts the moor
like an act of violence.
I cross by a hot-dog van,
scabs fall off my boots, a clag of moss
from Soldier's Lump. I drink sweet tea
in the mist, the next ten miles
are over a quagmire.
                              Strange place
to be selling hot dogs, I think.
Them nippers were buried out there,
the vendor says, turning his burgers.
He nods his head towards the moor,
we still get the sightseers.

So this is Saddleworth? I can picture
the gaunt, blonde murderess, smoking
a cigarette, watching the road,
Brady unrolling the carpets, cracking
puns with every strike of the spade.
He's a brainy one this one,
a right little bleeder.

I move on through the flutings
of peat bog, the drizzle of rain,
only me and the moss breathing,
everything else dead. The bleached
rib of an animal curls from the ground
like the heart of a flayed orchid.
Under my feet, the bodies of children
swim to the clear, sweet water table.

LILITH

She lay in the meadow sunning herself,
stroking the fine white hairs on her legs:
He ran to the woods to masturbate.

He found her again, up near His pad,
naked, oblivious. He had to admit, there was
something about her that drove Him crazy.

He walked towards her, turning a question
over and over, her presence unnerved Him,
He could barely speak He was so besotted.

What do you think of my garden? He said.
His whole body shook. Have you ever seen orchids
as pretty as these? Lilith opened her legs.

Have you ever seen orchids as pretty as these?
Touch the petals, she whispered,
feel how damp they are, how covered in dew.

He felt the springs pop in His head
like an old settee. He felt out of his depth.
Who the hell are you? He asked.

You can call me Lily, she said. *Adam's*
truant wife. Sweat poured from His scalp,
He turned away. This wasn't part of His plan.

AFTER THE CONCERT

Roadies took down the gantry, piece by piece,
carried the spotlights out of the hall.
The speakers were wheeled off stage
humming like beehives.

I told you I loved you, that time was short,
that moment's vanished without trace.

They slid the rafters out of the roof.
Someone was putting the windows into a van.

You said the music was almost gone,
that only a faint trembling remained.

The roof came off and the glow of twilight
entered your eyes. The walls came down,
the floorboards were pulled from under us,
we hardly felt them, we were so intent
on our kissing.

It was quiet then, we took off our clothes
and lay in the grass.
You said there were leaves in my hair,
I told you your skin was covered in dew.

You said it was funny the way things moved;
how moments passed by without our noticing.

I held your hand; you kissed my lips
and our voices moved seamlessly
into the past.

MY FATHER SHAVING CHARLES DARWIN

As he sinks his backside into the domed
seat of the barber's shop, my father
tips him back like a spaceman to gaze

at the cobwebs whiskered with shavings.
He strokes his fingers through Mr Darwin's
facial hair and tugs, as you might

an implausible stick-on beard.
Well what's it to be, lad?
Only a trim, a bit of a tidy up, says Darwin

settling into the chair.
My father pulls the clippers
out of their box and flicks the switch.

We'll have you looking like a man in next
to no time, my father mutters over the Brylcreem,
can't have you looking like a monkey.

His beard comes off like sparks on a foundry floor.
Need a pair of goggles for this job, he shouts
above the din. He dreams of shaving

the world's heretics clean of their facial hair,
Sigmund Freud, Karl Marx, Fidel Castro; doing his
own little bit for God and for moral decency.

He strops the blade, it runs in furrows
across the man's face, leaving the glass-like purity
that makes my father want to weep.

When the transformation is complete
he takes off the cape and brushes Mr Darwin's neck.
My father's eyes are filled with tears.

He's done a good job, he's humming now,
the tune of 'Jerusalem', stroking the shaven jaws
of Charles Darwin, who sits in his chair, petrified.

SKELETON

A skeleton propped in a chair with a party hat
set comically on the top of its skull, a pair
of green pants, a brandy glass between thumb
and forefinger. It was hot. The bailiffs
drew back the curtains and opened the windows,
wafting their hands in front of their faces.
After they'd checked upstairs and found
no one, they came back down to the sitting room.
Frank opened the drinks cabinet and poured
a brandy. A Christmas tree stood in the corner,
fairy-lights blazing, its white synthetic
needles a parody of snow and ice this hot
June day. He picked up the *TV Times*, three years
old, and read through the Christmas films.
His nostrils twitched, he could just detect
the faint, thin sweetness of meat in the air,
the hint of a nearby butchers caught on the breeze.
Bob turned off the fire.
It's a canny skeleton though, he said,
I'll take that home for the bairns.
                                      Frank shook his head,
he'd noticed the yellow moons of toenails
balanced on each toe, the glint of a filling
inside the jaw. He felt a ripple of goose-flesh
roll up his back. He finished his drink
and took a closer look. He fingered the skull,
buttery, yellow, he sniffed the joints
at the shoulder-blades: that smell again,
a trace of meat, a sweetness of fat.
He stared through the ribs, a cage, he thought,
with its bird missing. He wondered
where all the blood had gone, its colour
for instance. He made a cross on his T-shirt

and sat in the arm-chair, feeling his heartbeat,
feeling the sweat pour out of him, wondering
if he wasn't too old for this kind of work any more.

THE HUNGER

The night the bulldozers cleared the last
tree, Erisichthon had a troubled sleep
in his brand new house, smelling of oak
and maple. He woke from a nightmare:
he'd run his knife through the green man
they said lived in his woods. His wounds
opened like mouths, bloodless, clean
as buttonholes. Furious at this lack
of bleeding, Erisichthon tore him apart
like a Lollo Rosso, gorging himself
on every piece. When he woke at six
his belly hurt with hunger, his jaws
from chewing all night on his own teeth.
He stumbled downstairs to the kitchen
and emptied the fridge in a frenzy of eating:
a block of cheddar, some garlic sausage,
a mouthful of peas, a punnet of mushrooms,
even the wrappers, labels and bar-codes
were shovelled down, the sludge of watercress,
crumpled cucumbers, and the mildewed baby tomatoes
rotting away in the salad compartment.
When the fridge was empty the ache in his gut
felt worse than before. He cleared the shelves
of his cupboards, tamarind paste, a bottle
of Lingham's sweet chilli sauce, packets
of dried soup, and all the time, the inconsolable
pain of hunger. He went through the deep-freeze,
the chunks of steak slid down his throat
like bleeding ice-creams. When he'd scoffed
the last edible morsel left in the house, he grabbed
the cat off the window-sill, broke its back
like a stick of celery, de-stringed it,
and finished it off, teeth, pelt, nails, and all.

Nothing left but the worms in the lawn,
but he hadn't the strength. As the pain grew
fiercer, he took a long, loving look at the meat
on his arm and set to work without a question,
ripping the pink flesh from its bone,
even the pain filled him like food. He was so
ravenous, he became impatient with teeth,
they were too blunt, too slow for the job,
so he took the kitchen knife and sliced long
fillets into a dish. When the jugular went,
and he fell on the floor, the kitchen cupboards
opened their sores, the wood began to bleed,
the ceiling beams ran like guttering, even
the bread-board lay on the table moist as a sirloin.

When Mrs Ceres the cleaning lady came on Monday
morning, she pushed her way through saplings
and brambles to get to the kitchen. She found
a skull under the bushes close to the fridge,
clean as porcelain. The cracked ceramic
floor was covered in acorns, the walls were thick
with leaves and nettles. Well, she wasn't going
to clean this lot up, she'd have a cup of tea,
and eat her sandwiches. Served him right,
she thought, all that chopping down trees,
trees have feelings too.
The cupboards rustled with nesting birds:
sparrows, wrens, goldfinches. The sun was coming out
from behind the stove, she loosened her collar,
opened her flask, and stretched herself out
in the pleasant copse of his kitchen.

IN PRAISE OF SPARE RIBS

I rip the pork off its rib,
succulent, dripping with saturates.
I love this stuff. The vegetarians
would have us believe that every mouthful
knocks a day off your life
like a good fag or a bottle of beer.
I fish the plumpest out of its bowl,
my head fills with an odour of tallow
and suet. The flesh is tender, sensuous,
glutted with oils.
I suck till I feel the polish
of clean bone on my tongue.
When the last rib is finished,
I lick the sauce off my fingers,
pick the pig's hair out of my teeth,
rinse with a spicy Alsatian white.

THE BUDDHA OF ABSURDITY

Here the cow is a sacred beast.
She is chewing a cardboard box
in the middle of the busiest road in town.
She has not been run over.
We are stuck in a two-mile tailback.
She is teaching the Indians of Varanasi
the art of patience, she's the Buddha of Absurdity.
My rickshaw driver is apoplectic,
he can feel his precious petrol
combusting under the seat.
He could murder her, though he fears
his certain rebirth as a cockroach
more than that momentary pleasure.
So he sits with his hand on the horn
and spits gobfuls of scarlet phlegm
and betel nut into the road: the dust
is thick with it.
At last, she lifts her head, blinks,
and pulls her milkless sack off the road
like a drunken bag-woman, staggers
a moment, then takes a stroll
up the middle of the street.
She drops a spadeful of dung
the colour of sunflowers and wanders off
in search of something with a little more
chlorophyll.

THE MIRACLE OF DRINK

I can picture them now: doing their doctors' rounds
in the stifling heat, all day on the road,
the dust and flies, the parched throats;
you'd want a good drink. The only party
in town a wedding of temperance folk,
jugfuls of cold water stacked on the tables;
good on a hot night like that, but not
good enough for the boys, choking for a drop
of the purple stuff, and the nearest off-licence
halfway back to Jericho. 'Come on Jesus, give us
a useful bloody miracle for once,' said Thomas.
'Aye, get the beers in,' said Luke. He saw the sweat
on their beards, the sun-glazed looks in their eyes,
they could do with an evening off; could do
with a bit of a laugh himself, so he passed
among the tables, deft as a waiter, stroking
the jugs with his fingers. He carried one back.
What's it to be John, orange juice, beer or wine?
Wine, said John, and Jesus poured him
a cupful of sparkling red. *Matthew?* White for me,
and he poured a mugful of ice-cold Chardonnay
from the same spout. *Pure bloody magic, eh?*
Peter my son, what's your poison? Juice for me,
and his glass turned orange and rattled with ice cubes.
Judas? Any chance of a scotch, boss? *That's my boy,*
and he poured him a snifter of twenty-year-old,
dark as tobacco. *I'll have one of those myself,*
he said, raising his glass to the twelve
apostles, who stood around him, sweating, slavering,
waiting for Jesus to give them the nod. *Here's*
to the miracle of a good drink, he said, *cheers*:
and they raised their pots, and downed them in one.

THE SECOND WIFE

Since Lilith had left him, he'd taken
to buggering sheep in the hills,
petty theft, disrupting the peace.
It was getting on God's nerves.
He took the gear to Adam's place:
flesh and bone in a sack, jars
of viscera, bits of a brain, the skull
from a previous job.
Okay, let's have another go, He said,
one more wife coming right up.
He was full of booze, His head
swam with ideas.
He put the flesh on her bones, shaped
her breasts, pinching a half inch
nipple on each. *You don't get many of them
to the pound!*
He cut the gash between her legs with a wink,
patched in the hair, gave the kiss.
They both stood back to watch.
She tried to stand, but a knee-joint slipped
and she fell on her back in the mud, her mouth
gaping, her eyes staring at nothing.

BROKEN PROMISES

He was so late: he went through the village
looking for her, checking their old haunts,
but the streets were deserted, the only sound,
waves crashing the harbour, a foul night.
He turned up his collar and went to the pub,
they'd know in there where she was.
But the blank, sad stares of the drinkers
chilled him. Where's Phyllis? he asked. The barman
filled him a pint. A silence went round the pub.
She's dead, he said. *We buried her*
last summer. When you never returned
she was inconsolable. Demophoon closed his eyes.
We told her about the war, that you'd be back
as soon as you could, but she wouldn't wait
a day beyond that month you'd promised,
she hanged herself. The barman put a hand
on Demophoon's arm. *But look*, he said, *something*
weird grew on her grave, some say it's haunted,
see, on the table over there; we keep some cuttings,
to remind us like. Demophoon noticed a vaseful
of leafy twigs by the window; he'd never seen
anything like it, the leaves were dripping,
as if a rainstorm had just passed over them,
the table-top shone like a pool of grey water.
Them leaves 'ave been weeping like that
all winter, the barman said, *we haven't the heart*
to throw 'em out. Demophoon reached out his hand
to touch, lifting a droplet onto his lips,
he touched again and the branches buckled, flowers
pushed through the bark in a bluster of reds
and oranges, flaunting their stamens and pistils,
everyone gathered around with their beers, watching
the buds unfurl in the winter gloom, the colours

igniting in every pint. Demophoon sat by the window
watching the rain move on the houses, he thought
about Phyllis, how the days must have dragged
as she sat on the headland watching for ships,
perfecting her slip-knots, just in case he failed
to come, which he never would; he'd promised her that.

DATELINE

My boots were covered in shite from that do
in the woods, the bullocks approached me
near the fence, slobbered on my trouser-legs.
Such beautiful eyes, like hers, I thought.
As I came up the footpath a group of kids
threw rocks at me, one girl was laughing so much
I thought she'd choke on her ice-pop.
It's not her fault, I blame the television,
sets a bad example. Class talent though,
could have fucked her brains out.

When I touched her cheek, the smell of soap
came off on my skin, she was pretty all right,
couldn't keep my hands off her, sexiest mouth
I'd ever seen. Spunk written all over her face.
Just a bit mad, that was her problem.

I shave the stubble off with a care
I never used to have, scrutinise each move
in the mirror now. They say she cut her lips off
with a razorblade, don't believe a word,
it's just not possible. Gets to me though.
I check the clock, plenty of time, and anyway
shouldn't seem too keen on a first date.

I take off my clothes and sit on the sofa
before the mirror, like to look at myself,
nice piece of tackle. I make a tourniquet
with my tie, pull it tight around the base,
grow a cucumber, beautiful, smooth as a cosh.
A girl's best friend. I get myself ready,
brush my teeth, dress, open the *A to Z*,
find her street: not far, 35 mins, max.

IN ONE OF YOUR FILTHY POEMS

'I want to fuck you in one of your
filthy poems, crawl naked across you,
run my tongue over all the un-kissed
places of your body; the pout of your anus,
your armpits, the nib of your foreskin,
everything yours that I love,
in your girlfriend's bed,
her prettiest dress torn down the front.
I want it in print, so they'll know
how you move in my mouth, how your
million sperm, hot from their nurseries,
swim on my tongue, how I dribble them back
like a bird feeding her chick.
I'll bite you till bruise after bruise
comes up on your belly, thighs and chest.
I'll give you the only love-bite
you've ever had on your perineum.
It'll be like fucking in public.
I'll be so hot, they'll feel me come
on the clean, white pages, the smell
of our sex filling the poetry shelves
in Waterstone's, Dillon's, and public libraries
all over England.'

THE KING'S HEAD

As I raise the stamp's white gum to my lips
and stick out my tongue,
the postman thrusts a damp sponge
under the counter glass,
and says in no uncertain terms:
in Thailand we don't appreciate people
licking the back of the king's head.

THE EAR SYRINGE

The treatment bites, there's a gasp
of air: the nurse's uniform
spits as she moves, nylons hiss

beneath her skirt.
She shows me the plug of black wax
in her kidney dish.

I leap on my bike and head home,
with my fine-tuned ears
pinned back, receiving

on all frequencies. I can hear
the gasping of tarmac
under my tyres, wind unspooling

trebles out of the grass,
girls by the grammar-school walls
sniggering secrets.

I slip through traffic
sleek as a hound, curious,
hoovering noises out of the air.

I close my eyes,
and cycle home in the moth-light
of radar, picturing pot-holes,

taxis, pedestrians, slaloming
blindfold, all ears, all the way
down Peasehome Green to the house.

HUNTING THE MOTH

I go to the house of the Moth Doctor,
there's a growth in my abdomen.
He tells me to strip
as he mixes his medicines.

My skin comes off in a single piece,
a leotard of pink flesh; he dusts it down
with a camel-hair brush and hangs it aside.

We do this in a room of velvet,
at evening by torch-light:
searching my ribs for the infestation.

It hangs in my gut, trembling,
laying its eggs.
The Lepidopterist says it is harmless.

He feeds it honey
from a glass pipette, it suckles
and flutters its wings. I want it out,

but the doctor is crooning
and flapping his lips as if to a baby,
and after the honey, he feeds it bilberries
out of his mouth.

Timandra Griseata; he explains.
The Bloodvein, and he fingers
the dust on its thorax, then stitches
me up with a needle and thread.

One of the best I've seen.
You're a lucky man, he says,

and gives me a brooch of moth hair
to pin on my coat.

Your prescription, he says,
it will help you to see in the dark.
He gives me a jug of warm honey;
a bowl of bilberries covered in silk.

IN THE MEANTIME

Adam was getting despondent,
drinking too much, playing
cards all night at God's place,
losing the shirt off his back,
his last few chickens. Last night
he lost a goat he couldn't afford
to lose. If he didn't know better
he'd say God was cheating,
more than once he'd seen an ace of his
transform itself into a deuce
at the vital moment (though he'd
put that down to too much whisky).
They talked about chicks most nights,
how they'd like to shag the arse
off that Lilith, given half a chance,
tart though she was, how God
would magic a harem of them out of
pondweed and dahlia bulbs. But Adam
got maudlin as the nights
deepened, accusing God of negligence.
He'd been promised a wife, and all he'd got
was talk; he'd leave in a temper,
swearing, hurling abuse as he went.

THE WAY IT HAPPENS

The way it happens in films, the cigarette
goes out in the ash-tray as he takes
a last breath and closes his eyes. I know
he's dead, it is all too perfectly done.
His tongue lolls on his lip like something
still living. I hold his hand, rubbing
the amber skin of his fingers, hoping
to tease a last flicker of life.
I put my ear to his chest, it rings
the way a bell rings as it grows still.
Outside this place the streets are full
of the usual activity, a bus passes
the gates of the rest home, the sunlight
makes it so red, so new, it is breathtaking,
there's a woman on top combing her ginger hair,
as if there were nothing simpler, more
pleasurable. The sky is a bright, unblemished
cobalt, the trees are full of their new plumage.
I sit in my chair and watch him, the light
fixing his face on the pillow, sharp
as a photograph; every line, every hair,
the waxy flesh of his cheeks. The blue
veins on his temple. I draw the curtains
over the window and leave him: meat, brown bread,
nothing left any more. I don't care
to think about it, I pick up his cigarette
and light it, I can feel the cool damp
of his spittle still in the paper, the heat
of the smoke, then even that has gone.

THE BURNING GHATS

A scum of ashes floats on the surface;
funeral smoke, sweet with sandalwood,
rose, and patchouli. The corpses
lie in their whites, a queue of them,
up the long steps to the palaces.
Out in their boat, a family
are dropping their dead child
into the river.

I think of the Thames back home,
the black barges, the waste of a good
river. Give me the Ganges every time,
the bodies covered in logs and cinnamon,
a phallus on every ghat, black
with fingerprints, necklaced with lilies:
yonis – or cunts to us – with offerings
inside them, cows carried in silks
to the funeral ghats.

I like the Monkey God, the God for Toothache,
the God for anything you like. Not
the *One* God, the *Thou shalt not* God.
Sadhus contort themselves on the river bank.

Ever seen the Pope tie himself into a
sheepshank? Or push a knotted handkerchief
up one nostril while pulling it out
of the other? Can the Archbishop of Canterbury
syphon a glassful of water up his urethra
then piss it out again?
No.

There is no health in us,
we are all miserable sinners.

I count the number of mosquito bites
since morning, or maybe I should count
the spaces between them. Out in the river
a dolphin breaks the surface, then disappears
without a sound, without a ripple.

MÉNAGE À TROIS

Insatiable these mornings, full
of a drunk excitement, your eyes
have the glazed look of a woman
who hasn't slept all night; you wake me
with mouth-open kisses, the smell
of a different room in your clothes.
You take off your dress and show me
the stains on your skin
like the trails of exotic gastropods;
a body paint of semen
which I rehydrate with my tongue.
I trace the splash across your stomach
and over your breast, a thick dried
river of it, flooding again; your nipple
rough with a smear of salt.
That was one hell of a shot.
I suck on you greedily and slide
my tongue where his own tongue
must have slid long into the night,
and when all trace of him is gone
except the smell in your hair
we make our own maps on each other's skins
and we fuck like we never do
without this heat inside you, without
this ghost of a man drifting between us
like a lover sharing our bed.

THE ECSTASY OF ST SAVIOUR'S AVENUE
(Valentine's Night)

Tonight the tenement smells of oysters
and semen, chocolate and rose petals.
The windows of every flat are open
to cool us, the noise of our limberings
issues from every sash as if the building
was hyperventilating in the cold
February air. We can hear the moans
of the Rossiters, the Hendersons,
the babysitters in number 3; a gentle
pornography rousing us like an aphrodisiac.
For once the house is harmonious, we rock
in our beds; our rhythms hum
in the stone foundations.
                       We shall have to be careful;
like soldiers who must break step on a bridge.
We stagger our climaxes one by one,
from the basement flat to the attic room,
a pounding of mattresses moves through the house
in a long, multiple, communal orgasm.
The building sighs like a whore house.
We lie in our sheets watching the glow
of the street lights colour the sky; the chimneys
blow their smoke like the mellow exhalations
of post-coital cigarettes.

SOUFFLÉ

As soon as you said *soufflé*, I knew
we were in for trouble: and now
it has started. The mixture hesitates,
peeps above the ramekin dishes and goes
no further. You crouch at the glass front
of the oven willing them on.
Rise for God's sake, rise for once,
but like the Yorkshire puddings
they grow gnarled and stumpy, and you shake
your head the way a doctor shakes hers
when there's nothing more she can do,
and your eyes shimmer and fill as you
take out the tray of stunted soufflés,
smelling superb, but beyond saving.
I want to laugh, it is truly funny
to watch this comedy played out again.
I'm sure they'll be fine, I say
idiotically, and you tip them all
in the sink where they hiss
in the washing-up bowl.
The only time you ever got anything
to rise was when your bread ballooned
like the simulation of a small Hiroshima,
making an almighty mess of the oven,
which should have been
(as the recipe clearly said)
gas mark 9, to kill the yeast.
We put it down to your over-zealous
kneading, to your having done
something too well in the kitchen
for once, claiming a small victory
out of one more disaster.
So we sit with our chicken tikka masalas,

drinking the soufflé's inadequate
Frascati in sombre silence, broken
only by the oven's insensitive tutting
as it cools in the corner.

SCAMPI

What exactly *is* scampi, I ask the waitress,
and she stares at me as if I were mad,
but then, she's not so sure herself
and has to think for a moment. *Well*,
she starts, *it's a cross between chicken
and fish.*
         What!
As she walks to the kitchen
with our orders, I can see in the dark,
irrational part of my mind, chickens
copulating with fish somewhere –
the Department of Agriculture, Food
and Fisheries, wherever these things go on:
like breeding pigs without skins, or tomatoes
that last for fifteen years, turkeys
so large and succulent their legs
become arthritic and useless.
                      (Perhaps
if they crossed them with the prehistoric
genes of pterodactyls, they could hover,
pain-free in the thermals
like barrage balloons,
until the weight of gravity
brought them down for the knackers
to carve into joints.)
When the food arrives I've lost my appetite
and push the chicken/fish through pools
of tartare sauce, picturing sheep
cross-bred with dolphins: shoals of them
farmed off-shore, in grotesque,
woollen armadas . . .
             *For God's sake, don't
play with your food*, the girlfriend spits

across the table. She sticks a fork
into one of my scampi
and puts it in her mouth.
Dublin Bay Prawns, she announces,
absolutely delicious.

PREPARING THE LESSON

When I discovered girls, I thought it might
cure my criminal tendencies,
my obsession with shoplifting. It did.

I developed a more intimate need.
In my freshers year at college, I began
to filch the multifarious smalls

of the first beautiful girls I slept with.
I was mad with love for them. I carried
their knickers around in my pockets, rubbing

their silk in my fingers, all through
tutorials, seminars, final exams.
My lucky mascots, my study aids.

Now that my drawer is full to bursting
I keep it padlocked. I open it up
on certain days when I'm feeling old,

or love-sick for one of my first years.
They never give me a second look
these days, all P.C., good grades, career moves.

I push in my hands as into a bowl of water,
they are so delicate, sensual, as easily bruised
as the petals of new roses. It is like

opening a headful of memories, the smells
of bedrooms, perfumes, alcohol, the touch
of a breast, the brush of lips, an early dawn.

I hold the silks to my face, breathe it all in,
the names reel off in my head. I put them down,
lock the drawer and prepare my lesson.

SUTRAS IN FREE FALL

Fucking in zero gravity
is something else,
as Jan from the Particle Lab
ably convinced me.
We clung to each other
like sky divers, amazed
at such demulcent air,
the absence of weight,
the acrobatic grace
of our bodies.
I'd like you to come
in my mouth, she said,
the pump of her fist moving us
smooth as a punt; and I came,
unhindered by gravity,
in one straight line
like peas from a pea-shooter;
and Jan swam after them,
sleek as a dolphin
taking the salty beads
in her mouth.
I imagined them travelling
to Alpha Centauri,
the pearls of my semen,
moving through space
like a notion
in Einstein's head,
and we laughed at that
for a long time
and lay in each other's arms,
spinning like satellites
over the lab.

EINSTEIN ON THE
LONDON ROAD

They walk slowly these old men,
hand in hand up the London Road.
We always see them in our drunken
stupors; same corner every night.
Some say they move at the speed of light,
that they left the Conservative Club
years ago: it is only us
who are growing old.
They move like spacemen
through a different dimension;
by the time they're home
we'll be dead and gone.
The headlights of passing cars
sweep over them like days and nights.
They move slow as glaciers to me.
Juggernauts shake them like trees.
When I get home I look in the mirror.
I see I've aged, the clock on the wall
says 12.15.
It doesn't mean a thing,
12.15 doesn't mean anything at all.

YOU COULD GET ADDICTED
TO A BOOK LIKE THAT

The ache in my leg seems worse, also
that mole on my arm, swelling a bit I'm sure.
I drift through the bookshop
reading *The Family Health Practitioner.*
I carry it round like a priest
muttering a benediction for himself.
The doctor won't see me any more.
I run through the symptoms
of unpronounceable diseases,
horrors jump off the page: *fibrositis,*
AIDS, Mad Cow disease,
cancer, syphilitic warts, Jesus,
syphilitic warts!
I finger my flies and lift the book
to its shelf; it is only so heavy
because there's so much to catch.
As I turn to leave, every bone
creaks with the onset of osteoporosis.
I get scared, I think about the ones I love,
how will I tell them?
I hesitate on the doorstep;
I should go back in, make a few cross-
references; might be mistaken after all –
it might be something worse.
You can get addicted to a book like that,
the woman from the health section says as I
struggle it out of the shelf again.
We're locking up now, I'd go home
and forget all about it if I were you. So I do,
but as I limp to the bus-stop
I can't help wondering what it could be
the sales girl meant. Forget about what?

SHOPPING TECHNIQUE

I carry my basket through the slum
interiors of Gateway, past piles
of tissue paper, dripping like shovelled snow
where the fridges leak, past empty shelves
and bread stands, looking for discount tags.
Young mothers gang shop with day-glo prams,
filling their baskets with ham and vegetables.
Old ladies are sneaking bunches
of black bananas into their trolleys,
quarters of sliced haslet, tongue
and black pudding. All the best food
is nudging its sell-by date:
haggis, nicely ripe by now,
heading for meltdown, half price already;
trout in a vacuum pack, starting to mist
in its own white formaldehyde.
Potatoes are cheap, 12p a pound,
so I bag some up, and head for the tills;
a bottle of wine, for the trout, £1.99.
The check-out girl slides the items
over her magic eye with the slovenly
detachment of one who couldn't care less,
and who can blame her? The manager
grabs my arm as I step outside
and gives me the news in his best
management-training voice.
You're barred, he croaks.
When I ask him why, he goes esoteric on me.
I don't like the way you shop, he says.
And what way's that? I ask.
I don't have to explain, explains the Sphinx
of the supermarkets. I just don't like
the way you shop. And he leaves it at that.

HONEYMOON HYMN

derived from a Sumerian poem, 2250 B.C.

for Tim and Celia

I was mad for Dumuzi, I bathed
in the river while he watched.
I rubbed handfuls of perfume
over my skin till it glistened,
till it felt so good I could scream.
I painted my mouth with the darkest ink,
a lush, heavy crimson,
I finished my eyes in black mascara.

He wasn't graceful, more lusty;
hungry, I'd say. He opened my legs
with his rough hands, and crouched
before me, rubbing me up with those
thick fingers; they glistened
with all his work. I was ripe
as a Lebanese fig as he ran his milk
all over my lap, the sexy sod,
and then he was in me, with long,
deep strokes, and I felt him
break inside like a rainstorm.

Afterwards he oiled my boat
with coconut cream, caressing it
gently, as if he were bathing a woman.
She's coming up lovely, he called
as he polished her belly, stroking her,
stroking as if he could make her shake
in his hands, as I had done.

I took him to bed. I was hot.
Dumuzi, I said, when he could get no harder,
this is the one my cunt loves best,
I'll make all your days as sweet as this.
We played like virgins out of their clothes
for the very first time, ate blackberries,
got drunk on wine, spent the day
and the night in our honeymoon bed.

SOME NEW CREATURE IN PARADISE

The first time they met she was speechless.
So this was the child stealer Adam had warned
her about, smelling the rhododendrons,
walking barefoot in the garden?
Eve felt her stomach twist in a knot.

It was one of those days in Paradise,
seared with desert winds; they fanned
their faces under the chandelier
of an old magnolia tree.
Take a bite, said Lilith
offering Eve a side of her apple,
she shook her head, this was another thing
he'd warned her about.

Sod the boys, said Lilith, *it's only an apple*,
and her teeth punctured the skin with a hiss.
Its fragrance leaked everywhere, Eve
had never smelled anything like it before.
See, she said, *all in one piece, no fires
of hell, no boiling sores, no scabs*.

What the hell. She took the fruit in her hand,
fingered the cold, white flesh inside and took
a bite, the pulp hissed in her teeth,
syrup ran down her throat, so sweet
it filled her like an unfinished kiss; Lilith
was right: nothing, just her mouth watering.

They sat in the copse, the cores of apples
laid around them like early autumn, they drank
the cider that Lilith had made, held each other
like young girls, talked of their plans.

Around them, birds were pouring from tree to tree
like any other day, fish were jumping
for flies, flowers were shedding their scents.
The girls got drunk, their howls of laughter
echoed like some new creature in Paradise.

THE HANGING GARDENS
OF DOMBEY STREET

He grew tomatoes on the roof garden,
aubergines, courgettes and cucumbers.
His window-ledge sprouted lettuce and cress,
he even grew mangoes from his own pips.
He was sick of unripened imports,
especially tomatoes (which he used
for his famous ratatouille). He wanted them
blood-red, full of the sun, like those
he could buy in Provence or Tuscany.
The ones he bought from Safeway
were tasteless. This summer
was going to be different, come June,
his Holborn roof would resemble the hanging
gardens of Babylon, the tropical house at Kew.

But his prize tomatoes grew distorted,
their pips heavy with lead, dangerous
to birds and children. Once he found a whole
flock of scarlet parakeets
that had flown up from Nunhead Cemetery,
dead in his garden. His salads
tasted of rust, the ratatouille lay
like a barium meal in the small intestine.
There was something in the air, he said
dusting the soot off his cucumbers.
He let the garden run to seed,
lost all interest in inner-city husbandry
and took what he could from Safeway,
perfecting, eventually, a different dish:
his soon-to-be-famous fried green tomatoes.

A LIST OF REQUIREMENTS FOR THE END OF THE WORLD

A barrel of beer, two glasses,
a coal fire, toasting forks
and muffins, a little bacon, sausages.
Near the fire, a bed, a double bed
with cool white sheets, preferably silk.
Marital aids, handcuffs, ointments
and perfumes for later.
A porcelain bath on its legs,
Shostakovich's string
quartets, Northumberland pipes,
on LP (not CD).
Chocolate, lots, with a high cocoa
solids content. Waitrose is best.
Soft-porn movies, a polaroid,
some good, clean speed, or coke
if you can. A broken television
stuck in the corner. A radio jammed
on Hilversum. A girl
I've never met before.
A Saturday evening, dusk falling
in a flush of reds, and winter;
make it cold outside, freezing.
Try some snow, high winds.
Don't forget the radiation:
give it a long half-life, have it
come through the window in a day or so.

BLUE MOVIES

He was found in the early morning,
naked from the waist down,
by the cleaning girls
who came once a week in their rubbers,
flanneling Dettol over the seat-backs.
Nobody knew who he was, the doorman
had never seen him before, nor the whores
who worked the rooms upstairs.
A tourist perhaps. In his shirt
they found the stub of a ticket
from the Elephant and Castle,
dated and timed. The sell-by date
on his half-eaten sandwiches had them
wondering how long he'd been there,
unnoticed in front of the porno-flicks.
A couple of days they guessed. They found
a wallet inside his coat, with a fiver,
a condom, and a photograph of a girl.
The faint scrawl of a name: Robertson, or
Rolinston, was pencilled on a cobbler's chit
in his trousers, which were folded neatly
inside a sports bag under the seat,
with his shoes, socks, underpants
and a roll of toilet paper. They'd seen
it all now, nothing shocked the cleaners
anymore. *Dirty old pervert*, they laughed,
as the men from forensics boxed him up
and carried him out.